Idiom Speak 2018

HEATHER DURKIN

Copyright © 2018 Heather Durkin

All rights reserved.

ISBN-13: 978-1983632402
ISBN-10: 1983632406

No part of this publication may be reproduced or transmitted in any form (electronic, mechanical or otherwise) without express written consent of the author.

DEDICATION

To Joy, my English teacher

CONTENTS

11 Most Annoying Phrases 11
   1. Level Set 11
   2. Deep Dive 11
   3. Run it up the Flagpole 12
   4. Set Expectations 12
   5. Socialize 12
   6. Game Changer 13
   7. No Brainer 13
   8. 360 Degree View 13
   9. Best Practice 13
   10. Land and Expand 14
   11. Swim Lane 14

Acronyms 15
   C.O.B. 15
   C.Y.A. 15
   A.S.A.P 16
   24/7 16
   MVP 16
   ROI 16

Animals 17
   RABBIT HOLE 17
   THE FISH ROTS FROM THE HEAD 17
   BARKS BACK 18
   BIRD-DOGGING 18
   SKIN THE CAT 18
   HERDING CATS 19

UNICORN *19*
FAT CAT *19*
TAKE THE BULL BY THE HORNS *20*
DUCKS IN A ROW *20*
PRAIRIE DOGGING *20*
DOVETAIL *21*
VETTING *21*
LIPSTICK ON A PIG *21*

Apparel **23**
OUT OF POCKET *23*
AT THE DROP OF A HAT *23*
AIRING DIRTY LAUNDRY *24*
OPEN THE KIMONO *24*

Baseball **25**
TOUCH BASE *25*
IN THE BALLPARK *25*
BATTING 1000 .... *26*
BUSH-LEAGUE *26*

Boats **27**
WHEELHOUSE *27*
MISS THE BOAT *27*

Body **28**
ONE THROAT TO CHOKE *28*
BIO BREAK *28*
THOUGHT LEADERSHIP *28*
BLEEDING EDGE *29*
GUT REACTION *29*
PAIN POINT *29*
UP AT NIGHT *30*
FLESH THIS OUT *30*
FLUSH OUT *30*

A RULE OF THUMB *31*
SEE EYE TO EYE *31*
CLIENT-FACING *32*

Communication **33**
ALL-HANDS MEETING *33*
REACH OUT *33*
SAME PAGE *34*

Computers **35**
BANDWIDTH *35*
SANITY CHECK *35*
REAL-TIME *36*
POWER USER *36*
PING ME *36*
TAKE OFFLINE *37*

Culinary **38**
COMPARING APPLES TO ORANGES *38*
LOW HANGING FRUIT *38*
HIGH CALORIE EFFORT *39*
BREAD AND BUTTER *39*
DRINKING THE KOOLAIDE *39*
LUNCH AND LEARN *40*
SECRET SAUCE *40*
ON MY PLATE *40*
BEAN COUNTER *41*
BACKBURNER *41*

Fire **42**
DUMPSTER FIRE *42*
DRINK FROM THE FIREHOSE *42*

Flying **43**
HELICOPTER VIEW *43*
FLY BY THE SEAT OF YOUR PANTS *43*

JUMP *44*

Geometry & Numbers **45**
CONE OF SILENCE *45*
THINK OUTSIDE THE BOX *45*
CIRCLE BACK *46*
SPACE *46*
ON POINT *46*
ON THE UP AND UP *46*
ONE-OFFS *47*

Military **48**
ON THE BRIDGE *48*
EXECUTE *48*
ON MY RADAR *48*

Money **49**
PRICE POINT *49*
CASH COW *49*
Buy In *50*

Nature **51**
CROSS POLINATION *51*
GRASS GROW TOO LONG *51*
SEA CHANGE *52*
THROWING SHADE *52*
HAPPY PATH *53*
BOIL THE OCEAN *53*

Music **54**
ROCKSTAR *54*
BLOW THE WHISTLE *54*

Politics **55**
BLUE STATE *55*
RED STATE *55*
PURPLE STATE *56*

GET OUT THERE 56
GET UP ON SOCIAL 56
COURT VOTERS 56
RANK AND FILE 57
GAINING MOMENTUM 57

Sports (General) 59
RED FLAG 59
GET THE BALL ROLLING 59
QUICK WIN 60
ON THE BALL 60
DROP THE BALL 60
PUNT 61
SKIN IN THE GAME 61

Rooms 62
GLASS CEILING 62
ELEPHANT IN THE ROOM 63

Time 64
GOING FORWARD 64
GHOSTING HOURS 64
AT THE END OF THE DAY 65

Trains 66
OFF THE RAILS 66
ON THE RIGHT TRACK 66

Tools 67
DRILL DOWN 67
LEVEL SET 67
MOVE THE NEEDLE 68

Twisted Grammar 69
PUT THAT OUT THERE 69
"SO" TO START A SENTENCE 69
TO YOUR POINT 70

IT IS WHAT IT IS 70
BYE FELICIA 70

Vehicles 71
ELEVATOR PITCH 71
DAILY DRIVER 71
DRIVE FOR RESULTS 71
WHEELS LEFT THE WAGON 72
THROW UNDER THE BUS 72
HARD STOP 73
PARKING LOT 73
DECK 73

Preface

Welcome to the 2018 edition of Idiom Speak, a collection of some of the most common business idioms specifically chosen for the English language learner. New this year, is a list of 11 of the most annoying business expressions heard this year. After each entry is an alternative way to communicate the same meaning. Use this book when you encounter phrases that you do not understand when you work with Americans.

Idioms are confusing because the meanings are not literal and unless you know the inside joke or the etymology, it is often hard to figure out the meaning by simply looking up the meaning in a dictionary. It is also often hard to tell if other people find these phrases annoying or they actually like them. I hope this book helps you with your English language journey.

11 MOST ANNOYING PHRASES

Just because you learn an American business idiom, does not mean that you should use it all the time. Some of these phrases are overused and some are annoying and do not make you sound smarter or "in the know." They can actually have the opposite effect of diminishing your credibility, especially if they are repeated over and over again and used as a crutch. Following is a set of idioms that are particularly grating to the listener with suggestions on what to say instead.

1. Level Set

To talk to another person and make sure you both have the same understanding, expectations of whatever subject you are discussing.

Try this instead: "Let's talk about the plan."

2. Deep Dive

This overused expression simply means that there should be more analysis and investigation done on the subject.

Try this instead: "We should look into this further."

3. Run it up the Flagpole

To see if an idea is popular and get support from other people. When you raise a flag up a pole, it is more noticeable by people far away.

Try this instead: "We should get opinions from the team."

4. Set Expectations

To put limits on possible outcomes. For example, our developer might look at your code and tell you what is wrong with it, but he will not fix it for you.

Try this instead: "Let's talk about what is going to happen."

5. Socialize

To share information with other people on a team or in a company, so that they are aware of it.

Try this instead: "We are going to tell the staff about the report."

6. Game Changer

An idea that represents a shift in thinking.

Try this instead. "I have a new idea." or "I have a unique idea." or "I have a novel idea."

7. No Brainer

Claiming that something is such a good idea, no amount of thinking is required.

Try this instead: "This is an easy decision."

8. 360 Degree View

To understand all facets of a person

Try this instead: "This tool will help you get to know your client."

9. Best Practice

The best method to run a project or solve a problem. A technique or methodology that has a proven track record and works.

Try this instead: "The best way to solve a problem such is this is by…"

10. Land and Expand

To try something out and then use it more extensively.

Try this instead: "Sally is going to buy one bottle of the perfume out before she buys a case for her store."

11. Swim Lane

Often used in business process diagraming referring to the job or role a person does.

Try this instead: "It is important that everyone know their roles as well at the roles of their team members."

ACRONYMS

Speaking in letters instead of actual words is common in American offices. Most teams have their own business lingo pertinent to their own industry and specialty. This alphabet soup often takes a while to learn. Here are some general acronyms that are often heard.

C.O.B.

Close of Business

Sentence: "Please deliver this package by Friday, C.O.B."

C.Y.A.

Cover Your Ass. It describes an activity, performed by an individual to protect him or herself from possible subsequent criticism or in advance of possible future negative repercussion.

Sentence: "Nobody is honest around here. It's all C.Y.A."

A.S.A.P

As soon as possible.

Sentence: "Please call me A.S.A.P."

24/7

24 hours a day, seven days a week.

Sentence: "The client wants data 24/7."

MVP

In software development, this term stands for Minimum Viable Product and refers to the most basic level of functionality needed to create a workable application that can stand on its own.

Sentence: "Our MVP is included in the release plan.

ROI

Return on Investment. It a measure of profitability.

Sentence: "What was the company's return on investment on that project?"

ANIMALS

Humans and animals have a long history and it is evident when you start to analyze all the idioms that reference animals. Many business situations remind humans of their experiences with dogs, cats, fish, birds and even mythical creatures.

RABBIT HOLE

Originally meant to throw money away, but in offices this phrase is commonly used to describe a subject that is being thrown off track.

It is also used to describe a conversation that leads to nowhere but deeper and deeper tangents, eventually so far off course that it makes no sense anymore.

Sentence: "We don't want to send him down a rabbit hole because that's not where his expertise lies."

THE FISH ROTS FROM THE HEAD

A company rots from the top leadership down to the employees in the same way a fish rots from the head. This saying is an ancient proverb with an unclear origin.

Sentence: "Morale is down and it is probably not going to change if management stays the same. The fish rots from the head."

BARKS BACK

This phrase means to reference the source of something.

Sentence: "The strategy barks back to our mission."

BIRD-DOGGING

This phrase means to reference to a hunting dog that points out where a bird is located. In a business context, it means to seek out or investigate

Sentence: "Bill is bird-dogging that lead that just came in."

SKIN THE CAT

Let's achieve the aim or get it done. Originally, this expression is from an old proverb. Charles Kingsley used one old British form in *Westward Ho!* in 1855: "there are more ways of killing a cat than choking it with cream".

Sentence: "Let's skin the cat." *or* "There is more than one way to skin this cat."

HERDING CATS

This is a frustrating attempt to control a group that is impossible to control. It originates from the analogy that cats are not herd animals and trying to herd them is an impossible task.

Sentence: "Trying to get the investors to listen to reason is like herding cats. They are all selling off their stock."

UNICORN

Coined by Aileen Lee in the dotcom era who said that finding a company that was valued over one billion dollars was as hard as finding a unicorn. These days there are a lot more companies valued at over one billion in the world. In fact, VentureBeat has reported, there were 229 unicorns as of January 2016.

Sentence: "The number of unicorn companies continues to rise."

FAT CAT

A wealthy and privileged person. Originally meant a rich contributor to a political campaign. Now the common meaning is a greedy, rich person living off the work of others.

Sentence: "Look at that fat cat who has more money than he knows what to do with."

TAKE THE BULL BY THE HORNS

To confront a problem head on with confidence. It comes from the idea that holding a bull's horns is a brave act.

Sentence: "The CEO took the bull by the horns when he spoke to his staff directly about the company stock of the company dropping drastically in one day."

DUCKS IN A ROW

Well organized tasks and schedules. This expression may come from early bowling where pins where sometimes called ducks. It might also originate from actual ducks where mothers corral their offspring into a line.

Sentence: "He needs to get his ducks in a row and quit wasting time."

PRAIRIE DOGGING

In an open office plan, this is the act of peering over one's partition to look at something. A prairie dog is a type of ground squirrel that lives in holes in the ground and pops up from the ground to look around.

Sentence: "The office workers were prairie dogging and holding impromptu chats."

DOVETAIL

To link one point to another. Dovetail joints fit together tightly and are shaped like the tail of a dove.

Sentence: "These ideas dovetail together."

VETTING

To perform a background check before hiring someone. Originally a horse racing term meaning that the horse needed to be checked by a veterinarian before racing. Subsequently came to mean "to check."

Sentence: "Once the vetting process is complete, we can begin the project."

LIPSTICK ON A PIG

Idioms referring to pigs have been around for ages. A more contemporary usage is from Victoria Clark's 2006 book entitled *Lipstick on a Pig: Winning In the No-Spin Era by Someone Who Knows the Game* where she argues that political spin in harder in an era of transparency where the truth eventually comes out. This idiom means that making small improvements to something ugly does not help make the thing prettier overall. Putting a positive spin on something really negative.

Sentence: "That fix is like putting lipstick on a pig. The application is still broken and will not work for users."

APPAREL

What we wear is important. Tracing fashion trends back throughout history reveals ancient origins throughout the globe. For example, early humans probably wore animal hides to keep warm and keep the frost off. Here are some expressions have stuck around.

OUT OF POCKET

This phrase has come to mean that a person is unavailable. It was first used in this context in a 1908 O. Henry story, according to the Oxford English Dictionary. It also means to pay for something from your personal funds.

Sentence: "I will be out of pocket for the next two hours."

AT THE DROP OF A HAT

Without delay

Sentence: "I can be there at the drop of a hat. Just let me know when you need me."

AIRING DIRTY LAUNDRY

To talk about things that should be kept private. It comes from the idea that dirty laundry should be put away when you have houseguests over in order to avoid embarrassment.

Sentence: "Please don't air your dirty laundry in today's staff meeting."

OPEN THE KIMONO

To disclose information about a company or project to an outside party. This is a racy phrase. A kimono is a traditional Japanese robe. Social media strategist, Jason Chupick, characterized the phrase as "an unfortunate expression leftover from the dot-com VC days."

Use Instead: "completely transparent" or "full disclosure" instead

Sentence: "Let me be completely transparent about how this process works."

BASEBALL

Baseball began in America in the 19th century and has been a hugely popular sport ever since. These idioms are common phrases heard in the game that have made their way to offices. There are so many, they have been called out of the general sports and into their own section here.

TOUCH BASE

To talk to someone. In baseball, a player who is touching a base is not in danger of being put out.

Sentence: "Let's touch base after you come back from vacation."

IN THE BALLPARK

An estimate; a ballpark is an enclosed area. An estimate is an approximate estimate within a certain range or area.

Sentence: "Could you give me a figure in the ballpark of what you would be willing to accept?"

BATTING 1000

To do something very well. In baseball, a player bats 1000 if they make it to first base every time they come up to the plate.

Sentence: "He was batting 1000, when he got the standing ovation."

BUSH-LEAGUE

Amateurish. This term originated from minor league baseball fields found in rural areas surrounded by bushes.

Sentence: "That old website from 1996 is bush-league."

BOATS

The historical record of boat used by man is traced back to 4000 BCE. Ancient man used plants to put together simple boats. And we have been using them to get around in the water ever since. Here are some boat related idioms that have stuck around.

WHEELHOUSE

Area of expertise. Originally, a wheelhouse was a large house that covered the steering wheel of a steamboat.

Sentence: "Is coding in your wheelhouse?"

MISS THE BOAT

To miss out. To fail to take advantage of an opportunity. This is a metaphor comparing passengers not getting on a boat before it sails to somebody missing out on something beneficial.

Sentence: "We can't miss the boat on the next technological trend."

BODY

References to our bodies are plentiful in business speak, since we all have them. For better or worse, bodily functions and body parts have their share of idioms.

ONE THROAT TO CHOKE

Used to describe the advantage of purchasing all services from one vendor instead of two or more.

Sentence: "If the data disappears, there is only one throat to choke."

BIO BREAK

Term used to describe taking a break to go to the bathroom. The prefix "bio" means "life."

Use Instead: "Excuse me, I have to go to the restroom."

THOUGHT LEADERSHIP

This is another way of saying that the person is an expert on a subject.

Sentence: "Amy writes a variety of thought leadership content for her industry."

BLEEDING EDGE

Something that is so new and not thoroughly tested that someone might incur injury if it is used incorrectly.

Sentence: "That robot is on the bleeding edge of technology."

GUT REACTION

Going with your feelings or intuition. Refers to the gut or stomach.

Sentence: "What's your gut reaction about the presentation?"

PAIN POINT

A problem that is real or perceived. In business, entrepreneurs come up with innovative ideas by solving these problems.

Sentence: "What is your pain point with this process?"

UP AT NIGHT

What are their biggest problems?

Sentence: "What keeps your client up at night?"

FLESH THIS OUT

To give something substance. Comes from the analogy of putting flesh on a skeleton although not a literal definition. In business, this means to put details into a plan.

Sentence: "Let's take a step back and really flesh this out."

FLUSH OUT

To flush out is to make something leave its hiding place. In this analogy, details need to come out.

Sentence: "The process review will help you flush out your application."

A RULE OF THUMB

A principle or rule generally thought to be true but not based on science. Common since the 17th century, some believe it originated from an English law that said it was okay to beat your wife as long as the stick was no thicker than a thumb. Although, there is doubt that such a law existed and probably came from satirist James Gillray mocking a judge in the cartoon *Judge Thumb*. More likely this idiom came from the practice of using the thumb for measuring.

Sentence: "The general rule of thumb when making a sandwich is to use two pieces of bread."

SEE EYE TO EYE

To agree with someone and to see things in the same way.

This expression is found in the Bible. Isaiah 52:8 says:

"The voice of your watchmen—they lift up their voice; together they sing for joy; for eye to eye they see the return of the Lord to Zion."

In this context, the idiom is describing two people looking at the same thing and concluding they will agree on what they are experiencing.

Sentence: "We do not see eye to eye on that issue."

CLIENT-FACING

A position that requires an employee to work with customers face-to-face.

Sentence: "She works in a client-facing position."

COMMUNICATION

Communication is at the heart of many business expressions. After all communicating is the activity we use to work together.

ALL-HANDS MEETING

A meeting for all employees.

Sentence: "The all-hands meeting is next Thursday."

REACH OUT

To initiate contact with someone whether by phone, email, text or other means. To contact someone.

This phrase implies an earnest attempt to contact the person a little more than the phrase "I'll talk to Sue" does. However sometimes, it comes across as awkward especially when the speaker could just as easily say "I'll get in touch with her" and does not need to sound earnest or intense.

Use Instead: Call or contact.

SAME PAGE

In agreement.

Sentence: "Let's meet later to make sure we are on the same page."

COMPUTERS

Computer idioms abound in work settings whether your job is in information technology field or not. Smart phone owners are actually carrying around small, powerful computers all day long and even people who do not work at a desk most often have an interaction with some type of computer anyway.

BANDWIDTH

This expression probably became popular because in technical terms, bandwidth is the amount of information that can flow through a channel or the amount of time it takes for a webpage to fully load. It refers to the amount of time that a person has.

Sentence: "I do not have the bandwidth to write Ella a report on the state of the project."

SANITY CHECK

In computer science, this a quick check of a system to assure that the analysis runs as expected. It implies checking to see if the author was sane when he/she wrote the program.

Sentence: "You are my sanity check."

REAL-TIME

The actual time that something occurs

Sentence: "It is so nice to talk to you in real-time."

POWER USER

This is a person who is an advanced user of a computer program; not necessarily someone who can program but may have specialized business knowledge of the program.

Sentence: "The subject matter expert is the power user."

PING ME

A message sent to see if someone is available over text or instant message.

Sentence: "Ping me if you need me. I will be in my office."

TAKE OFFLINE

Used during a meeting when the discussion is getting too long. The meeting can be considered "online" in a metaphorical sense while "offline" is considered to be some other time.

Sentence: "Let's take that topic offline and discuss it later."

CULINARY

Everybody eats, so it is no surprise that there are a multitude of idioms resolving around American food and brands.

COMPARING APPLES TO ORANGES

Comparing two things that are not alike and cannot be practically compared. An invalid comparison. This idiom is referencing the distinct differences that one observes when comparing at an apple and orange. They are different colors, taste different, etc...

Sentence: "You are comparing apples to oranges. The problems are completely different."

LOW HANGING FRUIT

These are the most obvious or easily achievable goals. This saying comes from the idea that fruit low on a tree is easy to pick.

Sentence: "We will start with the low hanging fruit and then move into more complex problems."

HIGH CALORIE EFFORT

This idiom means that the task takes a high amount of energy much in the same way it takes a lot effort to burn a bunch of calories.

Sentence: "It will be a high calorie effort to document the entire project from start to finish."

BREAD AND BUTTER

Income or job that is used to buy the basic needs of life like food, shelter or clothing.

Sentence: "This job is my bread and butter."

DRINKING THE KOOLAIDE

To blindly follow. This phrase can be used ironically or humorously to refer to accepting an idea due to popularity, peer pressure, or persuasion.

It is a reference to the Jonestown Massacre of 1978. The origin of the phrase is more brutal and offensive than some people might realize when they use the term nonchalantly.

It is also common for people to think the term originated from the book "The Electric Koolaide Acid" test by Tom Wolfe where protagonist Ken Kesey and his "merry band of followers," the Merry Pranksters, drank LSD laced koolaide to transcend reality into a state of intersubjectivity.

Sentence: "Jan really drank the koolaide on the company vision. Every shirt she wears has the company logo sewn on it."

Use Instead: blindly follow

LUNCH AND LEARN

An event at which people bring their lunches and listen to the speakers during a lunch break.

Sentence: "Debbie is talking about productivity in today's lunch and learn."

SECRET SAUCE

A special feature kept secret by an organization deemed critical to its success.

Sentence: "We need to create the secret sauce if this company is going to succeed."

ON MY PLATE

To have too much work or too much to do.

Sentence: "I have a lot on my plate."

PAN OUT

Come to fruition or work out. It is a reference to panning for gold from the mid-1800s in the American west where the miner would wash gold from gravel into a pan.

Sentence: "Just in case the new job at the start-up doesn't pan out, you can always come and work for me."

BEAN COUNTER

Beans are cheap, so it is considered unnecessary to count them. Someone who is called a bean counter is someone who is overly concerned and nitpicks over small things in order to save costs. It is also a derogatory term for an accountant.

Sentence: "Don't be a bean counter over the number of coffee cups."

BACKBURNER

To put something on hold. It comes from the idea that the back burner on an oven is a good place to put a pot that needs less active attention. This leaves space for stirring the pots in the front.

Sentence: "Why don't we put the suggestion of unlimited vacation on the backburner for now, okay?"

FIRE

Fire was man's first technology, and still an important one. Fire can be lifesaving or life-ending, so the idioms relating to fire are definitely not subtle in their meanings.

DUMPSTER FIRE

A project or job that is a complete disaster that nobody wants to deal with.

Sentence: "That account is a complete dumpster fire. Leave me out of it, please."

DRINK FROM THE FIREHOSE

To be overwhelmed with information on a subject. A firehose is capable of spraying a large amount of water using bursting pressure in order to combat a fire.

Sentence: "On your first day of work, you may feel like you are drinking from the firehose."

FLYING

The Wright Brothers helped usher in the human dream of flying in 1903 with their first flight of an airplane. We still talk about flying with action oriented and wide-perspective references.

HELICOPTER VIEW

A broad view or overview like the view one would see from a helicopter in the air looking down at the ground.

Sentence: "I can give you the helicopter view, but not too many details."

FLY BY THE SEAT OF YOUR PANTS

To do something without a plan or experience. This phrase originates from the aviation industry where pilots who flew by the seat of their trousers or pants would fly without instruments, radio or a flight plan.

Sentence: "She just flew by the seat of her pants when the impromptu training was requested."

JUMP

To leave a conference call.

Sentence: "I've got to jump. I will catch up with you later."

GEOMETRY & NUMBERS

Geometry and numbers are all around us. These idioms center around the spaces where we find ourselves and things we can quantify.

CONE OF SILENCE

An imaginary object that prevents eavesdropping on a private conversation. Originated on the TV Show "Get Smart" where contestants had actual cones lowered onto their heads to keep their conversations private.

Sentence: "Let's get in the cone of silence. I need to tell you something in private."

THINK OUTSIDE THE BOX

To think in a creative way. This phrase is derived from management consultants in the 1970s, who challenged their clients to solve the nine-dot puzzle. Nine dots are arranged in rows of three. The goal is to connect all the dots using four straight lines without lifting the pencil from the paper. The solution requires creative thinking to solve.

This expression is way overused and would have made it on the top 11, except that it has been around for a long time.

Use Instead: "Let's think of something creative."

CIRCLE BACK

To talk to someone later.

Sentence: "I'll circle back with you tomorrow."

SPACE

Referencing an industry or market.

Sentence: "This is a new space for the company."

ON POINT

In line with standards.

Sentence: "I think Jim's analysis is on point."

ON THE UP AND UP

Legitimate and respectable course.

Sentence: "His offer for the car was on the up and up."

ONE-OFFS

A task or something not part of a regular sequence.

Sentence: "The developer is coding a one-off registration page this sprint."

MILITARY

Quite a few idioms originate from equipment or actions taken in the military.

ON THE BRIDGE

A conference call; a specialized type of equipment that links telephone lines; the bridge is also the command post of a ship when it is at sea.

Sentence: "Who's on the bridge?"

EXECUTE

To complete a task.

Sentence: "The program executed the task."

ON MY RADAR

To see something

Sentence: "The task is on my radar."

MONEY

Most offices are in the business of making money, so money idioms are pretty common.

PRICE POINT

This is a point on a scale of possible prices at which something might be marketed. It is another way of saying a suggested retail price.

Sentence: "What is the price point of this car?"

CASH COW

A product or service that brings in a lot of money for a company.

Sentence: "The custom blueprinting has been a cash cow for her company."

Buy In

Convincing other people of your idea or plan.

Use Instead: "Let's talk to the client about the new plan for next month."

NATURE

It is hard to ignore the natural world around us with all its colors and texture and beauty. References to nature run the gamut. Some idiom like "sea change" sound simply sublime while others like "boil the ocean" conjure vivid and dramatic images.

CROSS POLINATION

To share ideas from one place to another to produce innovation.

Sentence: "The brainstorming groups cross pollinate ideas."

GRASS GROW TOO LONG

Don't wait too long before you take action.

Sentence: "Don't let the grass grow too long on following up with that prospect."

SEA CHANGE

A profound transformation. The term originally appeared in William Shakespeare's, *The Tempest*.

Sentence: "The healthcare industry is poised for a sea change with all the recent innovations in technology."

THROWING SHADE

To insult somebody; This phrase can be traced back to the 1990 American documentary film *Paris is Burning* that chronicles the ball culture of New York City, and the African-American, Latino, gay and transgender communities within in it.

In the film, drag queen, Dorian Corey, explains that "shading" started by reading another person and is a dramatic form of insulting. Throwing shade grew out of "reading", and it is subtler. To shade is to insult without insulting. As Corey explains, "Shade is, 'I don't tell you you're ugly, but I don't have to tell you because you know you're ugly.' And that's shade."

The subtly of throwing shade originates from a place with no power and is incredibly subtle. The receiver can notice or not notice the shade. There is a nuance to throwing shade. It is sourced from an intent to exclude another person from something.

In today's popular culture, this distinction is a little more blurred, and people use the term to describe insulting another person. RuPaul's Drag Race TV show probably repopularized the term.

Sentence: "In the board meeting, the she threw shade on his idea."

HAPPY PATH

In computer science, this is the default scenario with no exceptions or errors and generating a positive response.

Sentence: "Let's test the happy path first."

BOIL THE OCEAN

To take on an impossible, ridiculous task or go overboard.

Sentence: "We are not trying to boil the ocean with this project."

MUSIC

Music is our escape, our emotional haven. Some songs lift you up, some make you cry, and sometimes we call each other "rockstars" at work.

ROCKSTAR

Being awesome. Calling someone a rockstar can seem disingenuous if management starts throwing it around too much. This term really should be reserved for outstanding performances.

Sentence: "Susie is a rockstar for staying late and finishing the proposal for the team."

BLOW THE WHISTLE

To report an unacceptable or illegal activity to law enforcement or other authorities.

Sentence: "Ed blew the whistle on the illegal gambling club operating after hours."

Idiom Speak 2018

POLITICS

Anywhere there are people there is politics. Here are some idioms are you will find it you work in American politics.

BLUE STATE

A state where a majority of the voting population vote for the Democratic party.

> Sentence: "That state is historically a blue state."

RED STATE

A state where a majority of the voting population vote for the Republican party.

> Sentence: "The candidate needs to win more red states."

PURPLE STATE

A state where equal numbers of the voting population votes for the Republican and Democratic parties.

Sentence: "Florida looks like a purple state this election cycle."

GET OUT THERE

Get out there and vote or get out there and campaign.

Sentence: "The mayor wants us to get out there and get the word out."

GET UP ON SOCIAL

Learn how to use social media.

Sentence: "Everyone on the campaign should get up on social."

COURT VOTERS

To visit voters in hope of winning their vote. "Courting" is an old term for dating, but this is expression is tongue-and-cheek and means to visit voters in their towns.

Sentence: "The candidate held 100 town hall meetings in an effort to court voters."

TURN THAT INTO VOTES

To use political capital and popularity to convince people to vote for you.

Sentence: "The candidate will try everything he can to turn that crowd into votes."

RANK AND FILE

The ordinary members of an organization as opposed to its leader.

Sentence: "The rank and file will stay back while the executives attend the board meetings."

GAINING MOMENTUM

To obtain an advantage in a situation. For example, in the Hillary Clinton versus Obama race for president of the United State, she argued that because she won some states she had the momentum but he argued he had momentum when he won 11 times in row.

Sentence: "We believe our candidate is gaining momentum."

BELTWAY BANDIT

Private companies located in the Washington, DC area that provide services to the federal government. Beltway refers to Interstate 495 that circles DC. Bandit is a comparison of these companies to bandits who shrewdly manipulate contracts in their favor and sway politicians in their favor.

Sentence: "They work for a typical beltway bandit."

SPORTS (GENERAL)

There are so many references to sports probably because they usually signify action.

RED FLAG

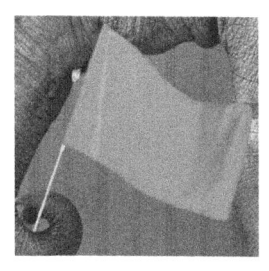

A sign or warning signal of danger. Red flags are used in many contexts to warn people of trouble.

Sentence: "We have a red flag here. The customer does not have the budget for this project."

GET THE BALL ROLLING

To get a project or idea started

Sentence: "Lacey got the ball rolling when she called the client and asked for their requirements."

QUICK WIN

A broad view or overview like the view one would see from a helicopter in the air looking down at the ground.

Sentence: "I can give you the helicopter view, but not too many details."

ON THE BALL

Knowledgeable; alert; It is a contraction for the phrase "keep your eye on the ball" which is advice given for ball games.

Sentence: "Cindy was on the ball and completed her project on time and on budget."

DROP THE BALL

To make a mistake

Sentence: "Joe really dropped the ball when he forgot to deploy the change set to production."

PUNT

To pass an issue to a coworker and avoid doing the work yourself. To give up on an idea. In football, it means to kick the ball to the other team.

Use instead: skip, avoid, postpone, or give up

SKIN IN THE GAME

First said by American business magnate, Warren Buffet, referring to a scenario where high-ranking people invest their own money in a company.

Use instead: "A stake in the result."

ROOMS

We all sit in rooms when we are in offices. Here are a couple interesting idioms about rooms.

GLASS CEILING

The barrier that prevents women and minorities from reaching high ranking, powerful positions in the corporate world regardless of their achievements. Originally used at the National Press Club in July 1979 at a Conference of the Women's Institute for Freedom of the Press.

In 2008, when Hillary Clinton suspended her campaign for the Democratic presidential nomination, she said, "Although we weren't able to shatter that highest, hardest glass ceiling this time, it's got about 18 million cracks in it."

Sentence: "She shattered the glass ceiling when she was elected president."

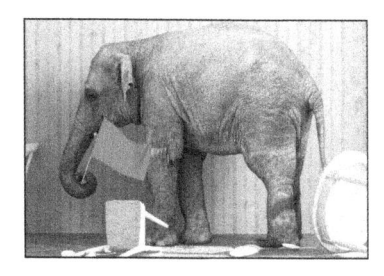

ELEPHANT IN THE ROOM

An obvious truth that is being ignored. It is based on the idea that an elephant in a room would be impossible to ignore.

Sentence: "Can we talk about the elephant in the room, please?"

TIME

We all live at the mercy of time. These idioms focus on the future and time boxes that we live in such as hours and days.

GOING FORWARD

This is one of the most overused expressions. It indicates a time in the future. The Institute of Leadership and Management has dubbed it one the most offensive terms.

Use Instead: "From now on"

Sentence: "From now on, we are going to meet every morning at 9am."

GHOSTING HOURS

When someone works a certain number of hours to get a job done but records a lesser number of hours on their timesheet. The hours that were not recorded are considered "ghosted."

The reason people ghost hours is to keep recorded hours predictable and helps projects make their margins on time and on budget. However, this practice makes new estimates on future project unreliable, because they are not based on accurate data. If the hours were actually counted, the manager has the option of writing off the hours which hurts the margin, or the manager can pass the hours along to the client which make clients unhappy.

Sentence: "Please don't ghost hours during this project. Record them all in the timekeeping system."

AT THE END OF THE DAY

When everything else has been taken into consideration.

Sentence: "At the end of the day, we work well as a team."

TRAINS

The first train was built in America in the 1830s, so these idioms come from a past where people thought in terms of tracks and rails.

OFF THE RAILS

To behave strange or not in the normal way. Comes from the idea of a train leaving the tracks or the rails that it travels on.

Sentence: "The client went off the rails with all the last-minute changes and kept the developer working all night."

ON THE RIGHT TRACK

Doing something correctly

Sentence: "The team is on the right track in their analysis of a potential solution."

TOOLS

One of the qualities that make humans so unique is our ability to use tool, so it should be no surprise that a lot of our business idioms reference tools for drilling, keeping things even and measuring.

DRILL DOWN

Used in a business setting after expressing an idea that may not be popular but wanting to see if anyone agrees.

Sentence: "I have some ideas about the solution that involves less time but more money. I just want to put that out there."

LEVEL SET

To review things, so that everyone has the same basic understandings and assumptions.

Sentence: "Before the project begins, we need to level set with the client."

MOVE THE NEEDLE

A needle was used in audio recordings to measure sound. In the business context, this idiom is referring to whether the action that has been taken is effective

TWISTED GRAMMAR

English is a funny language sometimes. The things we say barely make sense. Here are some idioms that fall into that category.

PUT THAT OUT THERE

Used in a business setting after expressing an idea that may not be popular but wanting to see if anyone agrees.

Sentence: "I have some ideas about the solution that involves less time but more money. I just want to put that out there."

"SO" TO START A SENTENCE

Starting a sentence with the word "so" has been a recent trend. If you use "so" as a response to a question, the effect is often alienating to your audience. It orients your message and alerts the listener that you are about to shift away from the way you have been talking. Consequently, if you are not actually shifting away from another topic and using it to start a topic, it comes off as a put down like you are talking down to the person. It is also an indicator that you might not be entirely comfortable with what you are about to say.

TO YOUR POINT

A way to acknowledge someone else's comments before adding your own. Used whether or not the speaker agrees, so may not be seen as flattering if the comments are contradictory. Easier for some to say than "I disagree with your point."

Use Instead: "Adding to your comment, I would add..."

IT IS WHAT IT IS

This phrase is used to describe the unchangeable nature of something. It is also sometimes used to excuse poor behavior.

It is a pretty flippant phrase; a darker version of "Whatever." Indeed, things are what they are. That's what makes this phrase nonsense. The meaning here is often an acceptance or a resignation of the object or situation as it exists.

Use Instead: Try to avoid using this phrase and instead decide if all possibilities have been exhausted and if so, just say that.

BYE FELICIA

A dismissive term that should not be used in a work setting but that doesn't mean that you still won't hear it. When uttered to another person, it means that the person should leave. The term originated in the film "Friday" with Ice Cube in 1995.

VEHICLES

From cars and buses to elevators and wagon, we use vehicles to get around and we like to talk about them.

ELEVATOR PITCH

A short concise speech about a product or idea that can be given in the time it takes to ride an elevator usually 20-60 seconds.

Sentence: "I'm interested in your idea. Let's hear your elevator pitch."

DAILY DRIVER

Something that is reliable that gets used frequently because of its convenience. It originates from the automotive industry where a practical and reliable car used for daily use was known as the daily driver instead of a car that was flashy and not practical to commute in. The quality of reliability is transferred to the object being described when this idiom is used.

Sentence: "Our daily drivers are our superior products."

DRIVE FOR RESULTS

Keep pushing until you get the results you want.

Sentence: "We drive for results, so the user experience is ideal."

WHEELS LEFT THE WAGON

This idiom means that something fell apart. A "wagon" is a four-wheeled, usually horse-drawn vehicle with a large rectangular body, used for transporting loads.

Sentence: "The wheels really left the wagon when all the data was lost."

THROW UNDER THE BUS

To sacrifice a friend for selfish reasons; to betray; bamboozle; A bit of a hyperbole in a business setting. Frequently used by journalists. Widespread use began in 2008.

Sentence: "Jackie threw Jamie under the bus when she blamed the system failure on his poor code."

HARD STOP

Having something scheduled immediately after the meeting you are currently are in.

Sentence: "I'm happy to talk to you, but I have a hard stop at noon."

PARKING LOT

A holding place for ideas that will get addressed later.

Sentence: "Thank you for your comments. I'm going to put those in the parking lot, so we can properly address them later."

DECK

Refers to a PowerPoint presentation which is composed of slides or cards. Not to be confused with "on deck" which means waiting to join a billable project.

Sentence: "Do you have the deck for today's presentation?"

ABOUT THE AUTHOR

Heather Durkin is a former reporter for US News and World Report. She lives in Northern Virginia.

Find out more at http://www.amazon.com/Heather-Durkin/e/B00XF4E6F8

Made in the USA
Columbia, SC
19 February 2018